THE OFFICIAL
HEART OF MIDLOTHIAN
FOOTBALL CLUB ANNUAL
2012

Written by Paul Kiddie

g

A Grange Publication

© 2011. Published by Grange Communications Ltd., Edinburgh, under licence from Heart of Midlothian Football Club plc. Printed in the EU.

Photographs © SNS Group.

ISBN 978-1-908221-26-1

£7.99

CONTENTS

HEART OF MIDLOTHIAN FC

Welcome to the Official Heart of Midlothian FC Annual 2012. This year's edition is once again crammed full of exclusive features about the Tynecastle first team stars.

Centre half Andy Webster reveals how cricket could have taken his career down a completely different path, while rising star David Templeton pinpoints his decision to go out on loan to Raith Rovers as key to helping him make the grade in Gorgie.

Kevin Kyle saw a rather different side to an Edinburgh derby when he joined the Jambos in the away end at Easter Road last season and he shares his views on a memorable experience as a maroon footsoldier in Leith. Strike partner John Sutton is also featured this year and the big Englishman tells how brother Chris sold him on the move to Tynecastle after his experiences with Celtic.

The U19s enjoyed a tremendous campaign last term, finishing just two points behind champions Celtic and one of the players to catch the eye was midfielder Jason Holt, who saw his consistency rewarded with a dream debut in the Clydesdale Bank Premier League. The teenager looks back on his big day at Tannadice – and ahead to what he hopes will be a rosy future at Hearts.

There's also a review of the best moments of last season which saw the Edinburgh club storm into Europe, courtesy of a third-placed finish in the Clydesdale Bank Premier League.

With many more articles, quizzes and stunning imagery, this year's Official Heart of Midlothian FC Annual is another great read!

WELCOME

CLUB STATS

The Heart and Soul of Edinburgh

Formed:	1874
Champions:	1895, 1897, 1958, 1960
Scottish Cup:	1891, 1896, 1901, 1906, 1956, 1998, 2006
League Cup:	1954-55, 1958-59, 1959-60, 1962-63
1St Division Champions:	1980
Record Victory:	21-0 V. Anchor Efa Cup 30.10.1880
Most Caps:	Steven Pressley, 32 For Scotland
Most League Appearances:	Gary Mackay 515 (1980-97)
Most League Goals:	John Robertson 214 (1983-98)
Most League Goals In A Season:	Barney Battles 44 (1930-31)
Official Website:	www.heartsfc.co.uk
Official Mobile Site:	heartsfc.wap.com
Official Store:	www.heartsdirect.co.uk
Official Online TV Channel:	www.heartstv

1874

ROLL of HONOUR

Roll of Honour Heart of Midlothian FC

Scottish Champions:	1894-95; 1896-97; 1957-58; 1959-60
Scottish League Runners-Up:	1893-94; 1898-99; 1903-04; 1905-06; 1914-15; 1937-38; 1953-57; 1958-59; 1964-65
Scottish Premier Division Runners-Up:	1985-86; 1987-88; 1991-92
Scottish Premier League Runners-Up:	2005-06
Scottish First Division Champions:	1979-80
Scottish FA Cup Winners:	1890-91; 1895-96; 1900-01; 1905-06; 1955-56; 1997-98; 2005-06
Scottish FA Cup Finalists:	1902-03; 1906-07; 1967-68; 1975-76; 1985-86; 1995-96
Scottish League Winners:	1954-55; 1958-59; 1959-60; 1962-63
Scottish League Cup Finalists:	1961-62; 1996-97
Victory Cup Finalists:	1918-19
Scottish League East & North Division Runners-Up:	1939-40
Scottish Southern League Cup Finalists:	1940-41
Texaco Cup Finalists:	1970-71

2012

EURO**VISION**

European football returned to Tynecastle once again after Hearts' third place finish in the Clydesdale Bank Premier League last season. Here we look back on the high points of the Jambos' campaign.

2010
SEP
18

2010
AUG
21

2010
SEP
18

10

AUGUST 21, 2010

Hamilton 0
Hearts 4

(Elliot 2, Kyle pen, Templeton)

After a draw against St Johnstone at Tynecastle on the opening day of the Clydesdale Bank Premier League season, the Jambos recorded their first victory of the campaign in emphatic style at New Douglas Park seven days later.

Calum Elliot and David Templeton set the visitors on the way with magnificent goals in the opening 45 minutes.

Kevin Kyle converted from the penalty spot after the break and when Elliot notched his second counter of the game courtesy of a superb solo effort, the Edinburgh club had wrapped up their biggest league win on the road for ten years.

SEPTEMBER 18, 2010

Inverness Caledonian Thistle 1
Hearts 3

(Innes OG, Stevenson, Elliot)

Hearts had to work hard for their victory in the Highlands, coming from behind to take the points against Terry Butcher's outfit.

The home side broke the deadlock when Eric Odhiambo slotted past Marian Kello, although the visitors levelled when Chris Innes turned a David Templeton cross into his own net before the break.

The in-form Calum Elliot turned provider after the interval to set up Ryan Stevenson, the former Ayr United midfielder making no mistake as he notched his first goal for the club to put the Jambos' noses in front.

Elliot then grabbed his fourth goal of the campaign when he got on the end of a Suso delivery to continue his superb start to the season, Hearts easing to another vital win on the road.

OCTOBER 16, 2010

Aberdeen 0
Hearts 1

(Kyle)

The Jambos' fine form away from Tynecastle continued in the Granite City as Kevin Kyle's second-half header was enough to bring the points back to the Capital.

After an evenly contested opening 45 minutes in Aberdeen, the big striker was in the right place at the right time to crash home a superb diving header just moments after the restart.

The Scotland international was proving a real thorn in the Dons' side and but for some desperate defending by the hosts would have added to his tally. As it was, one goal was enough to clinch a third away win of the campaign.

OCTOBER 23, 2010

Hearts 3
St Mirren 0

(Skacel, 3)

This encounter was pretty much the Rudi Skacel show, with the Czech internationalist smashing a wonderful hat-trick against the Buddies.

The midfielder set the tone for the afternoon when he opened the scoring and he doubled the advantage with a magnificent free-kick which he curled into the left-hand corner of the net. The crossbar denied him a first-half treble, although the Czech would have the last laugh when he finished off a move late in the game to complete the scoring.

His treble tops was all the more memorable for Rudi, as his third goal in front of the Gorgie Stand was the first time he had ever scored at that end as a Hearts player.

NOVEMBER 7, 2010

Hibs 0
Hearts 2

(Templeton, Elliott)

The derby bragging rights remained in Gorgie following the clash at Easter Road with goals from David Templeton and Stephen Elliott clinching a deserved victory for the visitors.

Temps smashed one of the goals of the campaign as he left the Hibs defence trailing in his wake after a mesmerising mazy run, the winger finishing his move by drilling home his side's opening goal in accomplished fashion.

Republic of Ireland striker Elliott netted his first goal for the club after the break when he got on the end of a Kevin Kyle delivery and any hope the hosts may have had of forcing their way back into proceedings evaporated with the dismissal of Derek Riordan for a late lunge at Rudi Skacel.

NOVEMBER 10, 2010

Hearts 2
Celtic 0

(Black, Templeton)

Three days after their triumphant afternoon in Leith, Hearts welcomed Celtic to Tynecastle and sent the Glasgow giants back along the M8 with their tails firmly between their legs.

Midfielder Ian Black stunned the visitors with an effort from distance, although he had a hefty deflection to thank for carrying the ball over Fraser Forster.

Not long into the second half, the match erupted in sensational style. Joe Ledley was shown a straight red card by referee Craig Thomson for a lunging tackle on Black and two minutes later the hosts doubled their advantage when David Templeton swept home a precision cross from Rudi Skacel.

EUROVISION

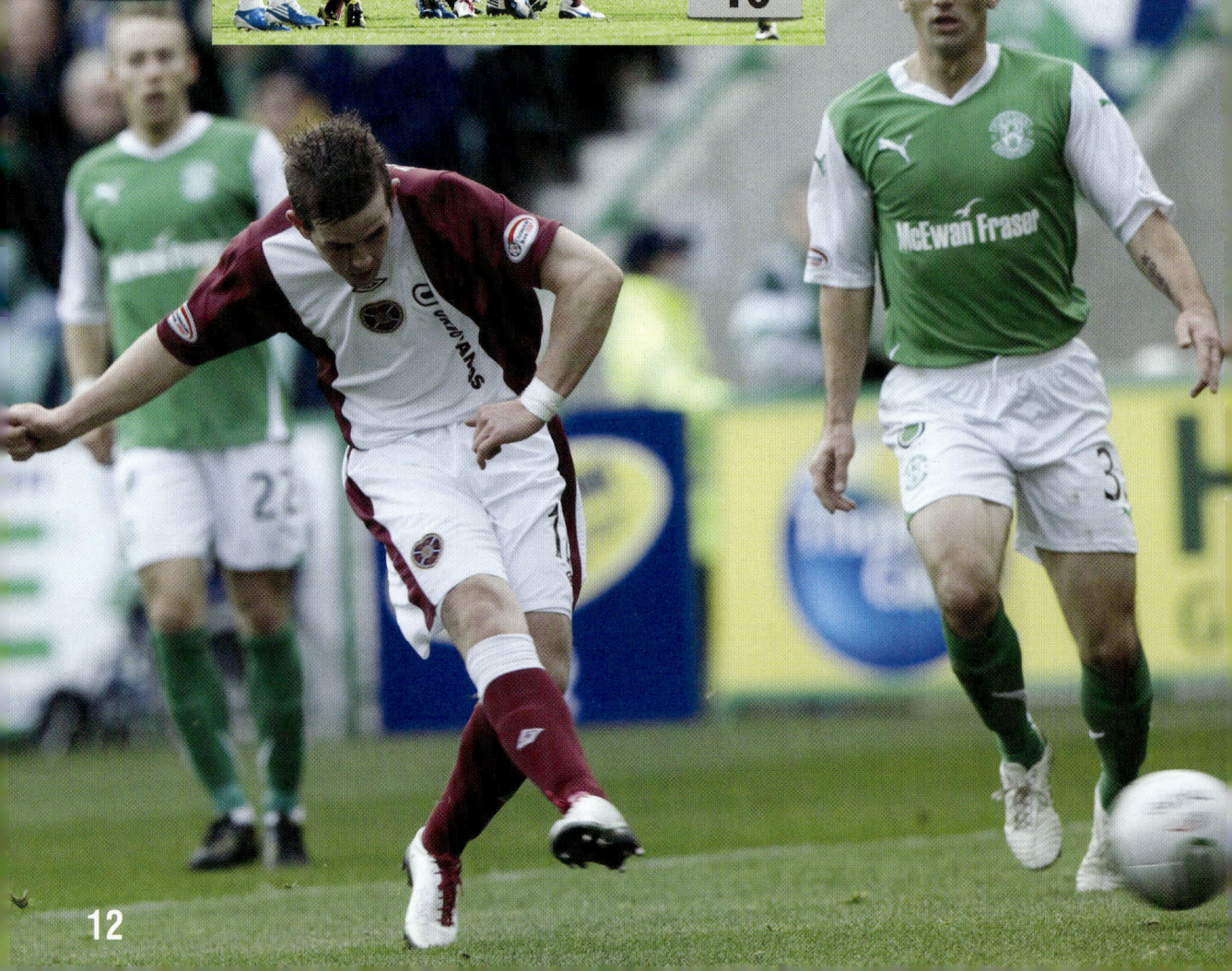

12

NOVEMBER 13, 2010

**St Johnstone 0
Hearts 2**

(Kyle pen, Stevenson)

Hearts rounded off a superb week with another 2-0 victory, this time over the Perth Saints, a result which carried the Jambos into third place in the Clydesdale Bank Premier League.

Striker Kevin Kyle broke the deadlock when he converted from the spot just after the hour mark. Ryan Stevenson came close to adding to his side's lead when he was denied late on by a sharp save from Peter Enckelman but the former Ayr man had the last laugh in stoppage time when he slotted home past the Saints keeper after good build-up play from Calum Elliot.

NOVEMBER 20, 2010

**Hearts 2
Hamilton 0**

(Skacel, Templeton)

Poignancy hung in the Tynecastle air as the crowd held a minute's silence to mark the memory of goalkeeping legend Jim Cruickshank before the game against the Accies.

Rudi Skacel struck for the home side just after the half-hour mark when he sent a magnificent looping shot over Thomas Cerny into the far corner of his goal.

David Templeton continued his rich vein of form when he smashed another glorious effort after the break.

The visitors were handed a lifeline ten minutes from the end when Iain Brines pointed to the spot but fittingly on a day when "Cruicky" was remembered, Marian Kello pulled off an excellent stop to preserve a clean sheet and complete a memorable month for Jim Jefferies.

EUROVISION

13

DECEMBER 11, 2010

Hearts 5
Aberdeen 0

(Skacel 2, Templeton, Elliott, Novikovas)

The home side exploded from the blocks against the Dons to set up a comfortable victory after a three-week break due to the weather.

Young David Templeton set the hosts on the way with an early strike and Rudi Skacel doubled his side's lead with just nine minutes on the clock.

Hearts had to wait until five minutes after the break to net a third, Stephen Elliott nodding home a cross from Ruben Palazuelos. The Jambos were rampant at this stage and a fourth goal duly arrived when Skacel was on hand to finish a good move involving Elliott, Mrowiec and Templeton. Arvydas Novikovas put the icing on the cake with a terrific right-foot drive past Jamie Langfield with 13 minutes remaining, the emphatic result Hearts' fifth win in a row.

DECEMBER 14, 2010

Motherwell 1
Hearts 2

(Reynolds OG, Kyle pen)

Hearts' purple patch continued with a sixth consecutive win in the Clydesdale Bank Premier League, this time the Edinburgh side sweeping aside the challenge of Motherwell.

The visitors got their noses in front thanks to a Mark Reynold's own goal as the interval approached, although the advantage was quickly cancelled out by Keith Lasley's leveller – the first goal conceded by Jim Jefferies' side since October 31.

Normal service was resumed just after the hour mark when Kevin Kyle stepped up to smash home a penalty awarded after David Templeton was felled in the box by Stephen Craigan. Any hope the Steelmen had of forcing their way back into things disappeared with the dismissal of Steve Jennings.

EUROVISION

14

DECEMBER 18, 2010

Hearts 1
Inverness CT 1

(Kyle pen)

The Jambos' magnificent run of victories came to a halt with a share of the spoils at home to Inverness but both Jim Jefferies and Terry Butcher were left scratching their heads as to how that was the case.

The Tynecastle outfit dominated proceedings but had to settle for a point after failing to make the most of a host of openings created in the 90 minutes.

The Highlanders actually took the lead after just a quarter of an hour when Adam Rooney forced the ball home from close range. Hearts were back on level terms shortly afterwards, Kevin Kyle converting from the spot after Stephen Elliott had been downed by keeper Ryan Esson.

Templeton hit a post before the break and despite second-half opportunities for Skacel, Zaliukas, Temps and Kyle, Hearts were left frustrated and had to accept just a point for their efforts.

DECEMBER 29, 2010

St Mirren 0
Hearts 2

(Templeton, Kyle pen)

The Maroons' march towards Europe continued with an important victory over St Mirren in Paisley as 2010 came to a highly satisfactory close for Jim Jefferies and his players.

Tightly matched for the first hour, it took a bit of brilliance from the in-form David Templeton to swing the match. The wide man may not have been enjoying his best game in maroon but he left the Buddies all at sea with a mesmerising run and finish past Paul Gallacher.

Temps was then the key man as Hearts made the game safe ten minutes from time. John Potter was dismissed after sending him crashing in the area, Kevin Kyle stepping up to once again convert with ease from the spot.

EUROVISION

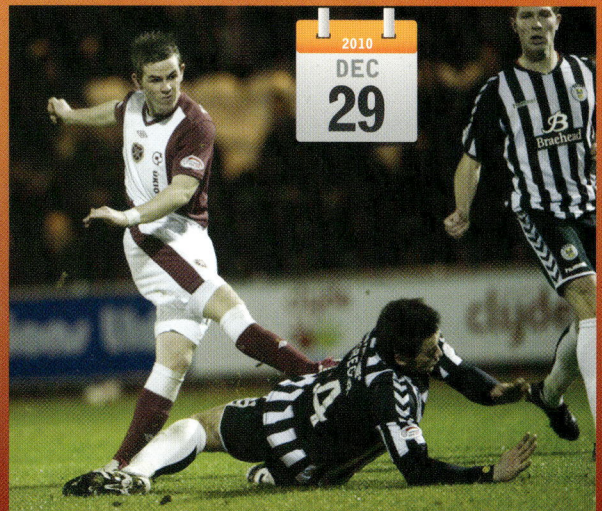

EUROVISION

JANUARY 1, 2011

Hearts 1
Hibs 0

(Kyle)

Tynecastle was packed to the rafters for the first Edinburgh derby in 13 years on New Year's Day and the home fans were the ones in party mood at the end after Kevin Kyle's late winner.

The all-important counter was set up by supersub Arvydas Novikovas, who danced down the left wing before delivering an inch-perfect cross to the back post where the in-rushing Hearts No. 9 headed home to send the Jambos wild with delight.

It was a memorable end to a thrilling encounter and stretched Hearts' impressive unbeaten run even further.

JANUARY 18, 2011

Kilmarnock 1
Hearts 2

(Elliott 2)

Jim Jefferies' men showed their battling qualities to come from behind and take all three points back to the Capital from Ayrshire.

Killie opened the scoring after 18 minutes when a shot from Rui Miguel found its way into the back of the net.

Turning round a goal down, JJ wasted little time in changing things with the introduction of Republic of Ireland internationalist Stephen Elliott for Arvydas Novikovas. And the striker made his mark in style, first equalising in the 73rd minute and then notching a winner three minutes from time to send the travelling supporters home on the long road back with a smile on their faces.

16

JANUARY 22, 2011

Hearts 1
Rangers 0

(Stevenson)

Those who may have doubted Hearts' ability to mix it with the Old Firm were given a wake-up call with this splendid victory over the Ibrox outfit at Tynecastle.

The hosts had Marian Kello to thank for keeping the game level at the interval, the keeper pulling off a number of excellent saves, most notably from a curling Jamie Ness shot which he somehow managed to tip round the post.

However, in a more evenly contested second 45 minutes, Ryan Stevenson popped up with the all-important goal with around a quarter-of-an-hour remaining to stun the champions.

JANUARY 29, 2011

Hearts 1
St Johnstone 0

(Skacel)

Hearts exacted revenge for their shock Scottish Cup defeat to the Perth Saints earlier in the month with a narrow win in Gorgie.

Czech star Rudi Skacel was the difference between the sides, his early strike from Craig Thomson's pass enough to keep the three points at Tynecastle.

The match was notable for the second-half appearance of Andrew Driver from the bench, the winger making his first appearance of the season after a long injury lay-off.

EUROVISION

17

EURO**VISION**

FEBRUARY 12, 2011

**Hamilton 0
Hearts 2**

(Elliott 2)

Accies were no match for their visitors as Hearts eased to a comfortable victory at New Douglas Park.

Stephen Elliott was the man who did the damage, the Irishman bagging a double as the Edinburgh side consolidated third place in the Clydesdale Bank Premier League.

The first goal arrived after 21 minutes when the front man sent a header from Lee Wallace's cross looping into the corner of the net. And the striker netted his second of the game moments after the restart when he deflected Marius Zaliukas' header away from Tomas Cerny.

FEBRUARY 19, 2011

**Hearts 2
Dundee United 1**

(Skacel, Zaliukas)

The Euro hopefuls served up a thrilling encounter in Gorgie, Marian Kello proving the hosts' hero with a last-minute penalty save to ensure a vital victory.

Barry Douglas headed the Tannadice outfit into a first half lead, only for Rudi Skacel to provide the leveller before the break.

Marius Zaliukas could not have picked a better time to grab his first goal of the season, his 87th-minute header edging the Jambos in front. The game, though, was to end in real drama when Ruben Palazuelos was red carded for impeding David Robertson as he burst into the area. David Goodwillie stepped up to take the resultant penalty only to be denied by the classy Kello – his third spot-kick save in front of the Roseburn Stand.

EUROVISION

Hearts 3
St Mirren 2

(Skacel 2, Stevenson)

An afternoon of high drama at Tynecastle saw Hearts leave it late to record an important win.

Behind twice to the struggling Buddies, Rudi Skacel and Ryan Stevenson's 81st-minute goal appeared to have earned the home side a point.

The Czech ace had different ideas, though, and popped up in stoppage time to supply a dramatic winner to help the men in maroon take a huge stride towards Europa League qualification.

EUROVISION

Hibs 2
Hearts 2

(Stevenson, Elliott)

Another pulsating derby encounter saw 10-man Hearts emerge from Easter Road with a deserved point.

The visitors could easily have been ahead by the time Ryan Stevenson drilled home the opener past Mark Brown after 22 minutes. The lead was no more than the Edinburgh club deserved, although the match was turned on its ahead when Marius Zaliukas was sent off after fouling Akpo Sodje as he attempted to latch onto a ball in the box, Liam Miller converting from the spot.

The home side eventually made the most of their numerical advantage after the interval when Ricardo Vaz Te slotted home 11 minutes from the end. But JJ's Hearts never know when they are beaten and Stephen Elliott smahed home a knockdown from Andy Webster just minutes later to secure a point.

It was to prove the first of five draws for the Jambos as they made third place their own and qualified for the UEFA Europa League.

VISION

Ryan McGowan

17

Spot the Ball

USE YOUR SKILLS TO SPOT THE BALL IN THE PICTURE ABOVE. ANSWERS ON P59.

STINT AT
RAITH
ROVERS
PLAYED
KEY ROLE
IN WINGER'S
PROGRESS

12

REGARDLESS OF WHAT HE GOES ON TO ACHIEVE IN HIS CAREER, DAVID TEMPLETON WILL FONDLY REMEMBER TWO KEY MOMENTS IN HIS HEARTS CAREER.

The first was his decision to join Raith Rovers on loan shortly after arriving at Tynecastle from Stenhousemuir in early 2007, a move which saw him learn about the importance of defending as well as attacking.

The second was his first start for the Jambos, his big day coming against Celtic in front of a packed Parkhead as the Glasgow giants went gunning for the Clydesdale Bank Premier League title on the final day of the 2008-09 campaign.

Temps was with the U19s under Darren Murray's guidance when the opportunity came to move to Stark's Park and the winger is the first to admit that switch helped mould him into the player he is today.

"One of the big differences I found when I came here from Stenhousemuir was the full-time training every day," he said. "The training was also a lot better and the facilities were a lot better too so it was all good.

"But going out on loan to Raith Rovers under John McGlynn helped me a lot. He helped me with my defensive side of things and that helped me improve my all-round game.

"It was really beneficial to do that. Having played with Stenhousemuir I was used to coming up against guys bigger than me and when I went on loan to Raith I had to get used to the fact it was not the U19s anymore, they were seasoned pros lining up against me.

"That played a massive part in my progress. It would have been great to see Raith come up last season but it wasn't to be. Maybe they can make it in the near future."

The 22-year-old marked his first start for the club by helping Hearts secure a 0-0 draw at Parkhead - his glory day coming after his debut as a substitute against Aberdeen at Pittodrie.

It may have been well over two years since he ran out the tunnel at Parkhead but a smile still spreads across his lips as recalls that May afternoon in the east end of Glasgow.

"My first start for Hearts came at Parkhead on the last game of the season when Celtic were still going for the league in 2009," he added.

"I was really nervous on the day but it was a great game to play in.

"You become a footballer to play in front of big crowds and when the big games come along, the atmosphere is great."

Last season saw Temps establish himself as a first-team regular, the increased exposure bringing with it added adulation from the supporters.

"I really enjoy being here," he said. "I played a lot more last season than the previous one so it was very enjoyable.

"I was encouraged to attack and when I get the ball that's all I want to do: try to beat players, score or set something up for someone else.

"If it doesn't come off, I try to just go again and again.

"More people than I have been used to were coming up to speak to me last season - it's nice to hear and nice to see people noticing that you have been doing well."

"YOU BECOME A FOOTBALLER TO PLAY IN FRONT OF BIG CROWDS AND WHEN THE BIG GAMES COME ALONG, THE ATMOSPHERE IS GREAT."

Temps Cas

ed In On Loan

19 Rudi Skacel

Tynie has lost his way to the stadium. Can you help him get home? Answer on page 59.

Maze

4

Eggert Jonsson

DERBY PHOTO SPECIAL

2010 NOV 07

2011 JAN 01

2011 APR 03

HIBS 0   HEARTS 2

HEARTS 1   HIBS 0

HIBS 2   HEARTS 2

1. In what season did Mark de Vries smash four goals past Hibs on his Tynecastle debut?

2. What former Hearts midfield star was appointed manager of Cowdenbeath in the summer?

3. Which Royal visitors graced the Tynecastle turf in July?

4. Christophe Berra moved to which English Premier League club from Hearts?

5. Danny Grainger joined Hearts from which SPL rival?

6. What is the nationality of Ryan McGowan?

7. Who did John Robertson succeed as Hearts manager?

8. Iain Ferguson scored the winner against which European giant in 1989?

9. True or False. Andy Webster was born in Arboath.

10. In what year was the first game played at Tynecastle Stadium?

Quiz

H·M F·C 1874

Answers on page 59.

10 Stephen Elliott

12

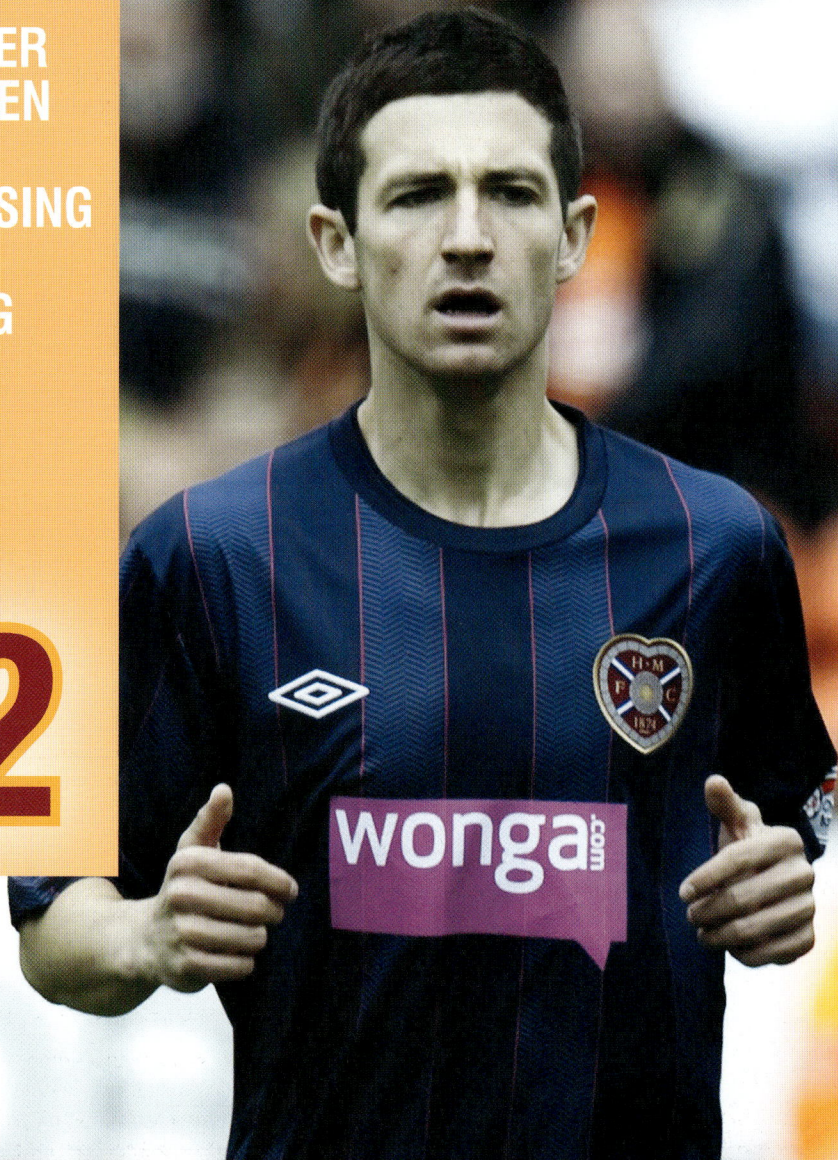

Worth The Wait

RISING STAR JASON HOLT SPENT HALF HIS LIFE DREAMING OF HIS HEARTS DEBUT - AND SAW HIS BIG DAY ARRIVE AT TANNADICE LAST SEASON.

With European qualification already secured, the 18-year-old was given the nod in the last game of the season as Jim Jefferies took the opportunity to give some of his top youngsters an outing.

And although the midfielder saw barely 10 minutes of action from the bench against the Tangerines, he insisted the wait was well worth it.

"I signed for Hearts from my local team Musselburgh Windsor when I was nine years old and have come through all the age groups," he said.

"To make my debut at 18 was a great experience and I just want to keep progressing. I have been with Hearts since I was nine so to make my debut at the age of 18 was really special. Although I only got 10 minutes, I didn't mind at all - I'd have been delighted with two minutes!"

Recalling the moment he was told he was going to be involved against United, Jason said: "I went in on the Saturday and found I was in the squad and trained with the first team. I travelled to Tannadice on the Sunday and that's when I was told I was on the bench.

"I wasn't sure if I was going to get on but when the gaffer told me to get ready, that's when it kicked in and the excitement really started.

"When I got on, that's when I was able to relax and play a bit. It was a great day to get my debut as that's what I have always wanted to do.

"I was on the phone to my dad on the bus home from Dundee telling him all about it and to be honest I was excited about what I had done for about a week afterwards.

"I've kept the DVD of the game and my top from the match, although I don't think our kit man was too happy!"

Highly-rated by everyone at the Football Academy, the Musselburgh lad saw a terrific season crowned with the Clydesdable Bank U19 Player of the Year, the youngster picking up his award at a glittering ceremony in Glasgow in May.

"The U19s had a great season last season and we were unlucky not to win the league title, finishing just behind Celtic in second place," he said. "The overall award from the Clydesdale Bank was a real boost and it's good to know opposition coaches recognised I was doing well.

"I can still play for the U19s this season but hope to push on and get a few more opportunities. I just need to wait and see what happens."

Level-headed Jason didn't get carried away with his promotion, stressing he hasn't achieved anything yet.

He said: "Some of my pals laugh at me calling me a 'Billy Big' as I'm in the first team but I don't think of myself like that at all.

"As far as I am concerned, I'm an U19 player. I haven't achieved anything yet and have only had a glimpse of what might come in the future as regards the first team.

"Hopefully if I can keep working hard, it will become a reality."

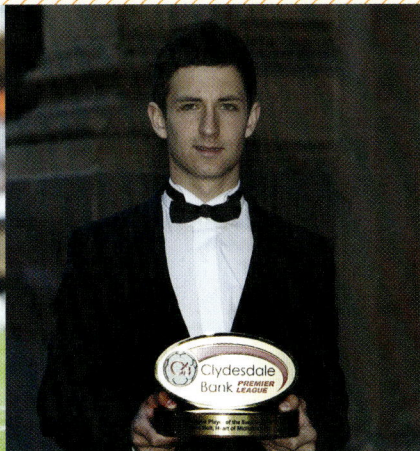

CHAT WITH BROTHER CHRIS SOLD STRIKER ON HIS MOVE TO HEARTS.

12

Tynie's Sutton Special

Strike star John Sutton reckons he'll LOVE his time at Hearts because his brother Chris HATED playing at Tynecastle.

The summer signing spoke to the former Celtic forward before agreeing to join the Jambos and he admits it didn't take long for him to be convinced that Gorgie was the place for him.

The 27-year-old penned a three-year deal at the end of May after a successful time at Motherwell and is looking to bang in his fair share of goals in maroon as well.

"It wasn't an easy decision to make on the basis I had always had a good time at Motherwell," said John.

"Once the gaffer here had made his interest known, it was hard to turn down the chance.

"I spoke to my brother Chris about things and he said he hated playing here as it was always very hostile and always a very tough team to face.

"So as much as he didn't like playing here, he highly recommended coming and he said it would be a good move for me."

Having spoken to a number of people shortly after completing his move, John admits he feels privileged to be at Tynecastle.

"Plenty of people I have spoken to said they wished they were in my position so I feel very lucky to be here," he added.

"I have been lucky to play here on many occasions before I signed. It is a great club and a tremendous place to play your football and I'm looking forward to forwarding my career.

"From our point of view it was a tremendous achievement to finish third last season and I know a lot of people were really disappointed not to get a good run in the cup.

"Hopefully we can do that this time and I can pick up a few goals in the process."

UNSUCCESSFUL CRICKET TRIAL AT DURHAM MEANT FOOTBALL WAS THE FOCUS FOR WEBBY.

12

Howzat!

DEFENDER ANDY WEBSTER HAS ESTABLISHED HIMSELF AS ONE OF THE KEY MEN AT THE CENTRE OF HEARTS' REARGUARD AND IS A RECOGNISED INTERNATIONAL FOOTBALLER. HOWEVER, HAD LADY LUCK SMILED ON HIM DIFFERENTLY, THE TYNECASTLE STAR COULD HAVE BEEN PURSUING A QUITE DIFFERENT SPORTING CAREER.

As a youngster growing up in Arbroath, the local cricket club played a significant part in his adolescent years, Andy spending many happy hours in the nets at Lochlands Park.

Such was his promise, he was offered a trial with Durham at the age of 13 and although nothing emerged from his stint at Chester-Le-Street, the centre-half knows it might not have taken much for him to be pulling on his whites rather than the famous maroon jersey.

"First and foremost football was the sport I had a passion for but I played cricket as well when I was growing up. I think I started in Primary 4 and played throughout school and really enjoyed it," he said.

"It was batting to start with but then I became more a wicket-keeper/batsman.

"Most of my life back then was spent at the cricket club in Arbroath, playing and watching during the summer holidays with a lot of other folk. Basically a lot of my childhood was spent there and it played an important role, particularly from a socialising point of view.

"When I was 13 I had a trial at Durham but nothing materialised, and let's face it there aren't too many Scots who have made their mark in English county cricket.

"It was good at the time and it was nice to get some recognition for doing well.

"If the trial had gone differently maybe my sporting career would have been different. Who knows? It's like anything when you succeed more in one than the other, your attention will focus on that thing.

"I signed schoolboy forms with Arbroath just before I was 16 so from that point onwards cricket slowly tailed off a bit so it was a natural sort of progression into football.

"I still spent a lot of the time at the club, though, because as a young boy growing up, it was a great place for me to be."

Andy's dedication to the game of football has certainly paid off, leaving him with no regrets over his choice of career path.

Now in his second spell at Hearts, he feels he has a major role to play in the development of some of the club's rising stars - in a similar way to how he benefited from being around experenced professionals on his arrival in Gorgie from Gayfield.

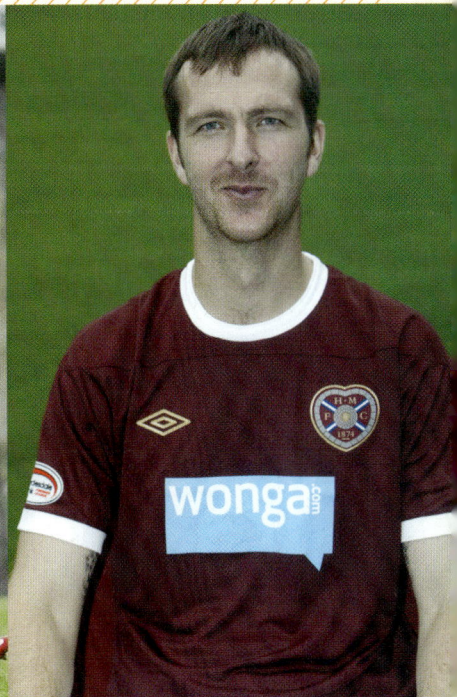

Howzat!

"The last time I was here I had a great experience and progressed so much as a footballer and a person," he said. "Since being away, I have experienced a lot more, progressed as a player and matured as a person.

"The older you get the more experienced you become. The shoe is on the other foot for me now as when I arrived here the first time I was always looking up to the bigger, more experienced players and trying to learn from them, from the training to the match day itself.

"There were a lot of older players like Robert Tomaschek, Thomas Flogel and Stephane Adam. It wasn't a case of having to speak to them all the time, I could learn from just watching them in training every day and subconsciously picking things up.

"I am at the stage now that hopefully the younger boys can look at me as one of the older statesmen in the team: whether that means if I do my job properly on a Saturday they say they are glad they are playing alongside me, or if they need advice on anything, I am happy to pass on my knowledge to benefit them."

Can you find these ten strikers who used to
play for Hearts hidden in the grid? Answers on page 59.

ADAM
ROBERTSON
FORD
CONN
CRABBE
DE VRIES
BONE
BAULD
BATTLES
KIRK

WORDSEARCH

WORDSEARCH

Y	G	E	N	O	B	T	D	L	H
S	M	Z	L	C	H	E	M	N	K
E	A	T	D	K	V	F	O	R	D
L	D	T	H	R	K	S	I	K	N
T	A	C	I	N	T	K	C	R	J
T	D	E	O	R	L	D	R	N	Y
A	S	L	E	N	Q	G	A	M	Z
B	K	B	U	M	N	X	B	B	J
M	O	G	T	A	T	J	B	V	Y
R	Y	D	D	M	B	N	E	Q	J

3

Danny Grainger

35
DENIS PRYCHYNENKO

He was very raw when he first arrived here and always seemed to be on his backside at training, sliding into tackles.

He had a bit to go back then if I'm being honest and we took a wee chance with him but he certainly came through that well. He has a good future in front of him and his ability to strike the ball as well as he does at set plays is a great thing to have in your locker. He is a good size and passes the ball well. He works continuously on his development and his decision-making on the ball is a lot better now. He is a top prospect.

DENIS PRYCHYNENKO

Ones to Watch!

DARREN MURRAY KNOWS THE HEARTS YOUNGSTERS BETTER THAN ANYONE AND HERE HE GIVES HIS VERDICT ON FOUR OF THE CLUB'S RISING STARS.

49
KEVIN McHATTIE

A Scotland U19 international, he came here from Dunfermline and he's what you'd call a marauding left-back who loves to get forward which suits the way the 19s play.

He defends well but also gets beyond the midfielders and strikers when we're on the ball. He's a great outlet for the team.

KEVIN McHATTIE

43

DAVIE SMITH

In my opinion he's a very good player, albeit he has a bit still to go. Like a lot of our U19s, he's technically gifted and reasonably quick.

He has to build up his strength a bit but his experience of playing for the first team against Dundee United in the final game of last season will have been of great benefit to him. He has a good eye for a goal and his link-up play is excellent.

DAVIE
SMITH

40

COLIN HAMILTON

Colin's a left-sided centre back and the last one we had like that was Christophe Berra.

He's not quite as physical or quick but what he does have is a great left foot and he uses the ball from the back very well. He has the physical attributes for the game here and he just has to work a wee bit on his pace. He knows the game, knows the position and has a wee chance of doing well in football.

COLIN
HAMILTON

1

2

3

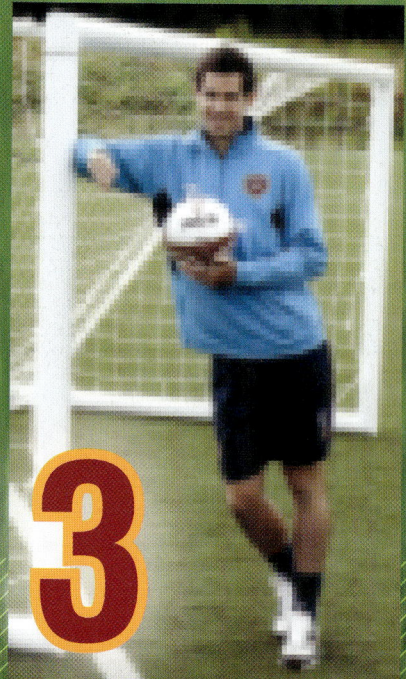

CAN YOU MAKE
OUT THESE HEARTS
FAVOURITES?
ANSWERS ON PAGE 59.

Guess Who?

46

Q&A

with Jamie Hamill

Is it true you made your debut for Kilmarnock against Hearts at Tynecastle?
Yes, Jim Jefferies was the manager in charge at the time and he gave me my big chance.

Can you put into words what it felt like?
It was a strange day, really. I wasn't in the team on the Friday but on the Saturday morning somebody was feeling a wee niggle and the gaffer pulled me aside at the hotel before the game and told me I would be starting. I thought to myself, 'wait a minute, I've watched Tynecastle on the TV and the crowd are right on top of you…' It actually spurred me on a bit and it was a fantastic day.

What was the score?
Thanks for asking! It was really good to make my debut at Tynecastle but unfortunately we got beat 1-0.

How many seasons were you at Rugby Park?
I was seven years at Killie and so it was always going to be a bit of a wrench to leave.

Given where you made your debut, maybe it was written in the stars you would end up here!
It's funny how these things happen in football and there's no doubt it's a special place to play. I was delighted to be able to join a club of Hearts' stature. It is a massive club.

Did you think about your Killie debut after agreeing to join Hearts?
When I heard about Hearts' interest, it got me thinking about making my debut and the all the other times I've played at Tynecastle. It was always a difficult placc to come for opposing teams and the atmosphere really feeds down to the players on the pitch.

What was the banter like when you met your new team-mates?
There is always a bit of banter after you sign for a club. It happens everywhere.

How big a step up is this for you?
It's a new challenge for me, a new working environment and working with new people. I would say it has to be the biggest challenge to date for me.

What are your targets now that you're a Jambo?
Hopefully to get some silverwear and challenge at the top of the league as I never managed to achieve that at Killie. Joining Hearts will hopefully give me that opportunity. I have signed a three-year contract and just want to try to make an impact and bolster the team.

KEVIN KYLE LOVED WATCHING THE DERBY AS A HEARTS FAN AT EASTER ROAD – BUT IT STILL DOESN'T BEAT PLAYING.

STRIKER KEVIN KYLE WAS GIVEN A UNIQUE PERSPECTIVE OF THE EDINBURGH DERBY AT EASTER ROAD LAST SEASON WHEN HE STOOD SHOULDER TO SHOULDER WITH THE GORGIE FAITHFUL.

Ruled out by injury, the target man decided to don his maroon scarf and take his seat in the away end to cheer his team-mates on.

Alongside Icelandic international Eggert Jonsson, the pair watched the drama unfold from the south stand. And the front man is the first to admit the Capital encounter made a big impression, all thanks to the rousing finale which saw his good pal Stephen Elliott grab a late leveller for the 10-man Jambos.

"As a spectator I am awful as I curse and swear in the stands telling the guys they should have played this pass or that pass," said Kevin.

"You see the game so much better from the stands but I'm not great at watching. I can't control myself and start arguing with the fans!

"The Edinburgh derby is unique, that's for sure. I enjoyed being in with the crowd, they were asking for photographs and autographs and I think they appreciated me being in there with them."

Ryan Stevenson had put Hearts in the driving seat in the April clash, with a well taken finish in the first half. The match, though, was turned on its head with the dismissal of Marius Zaliukas before the break when he was penalised for a foul in the area, Liam Miller converting from the spot.

Fan-tastic!

**KEVIN
KYLE**

9

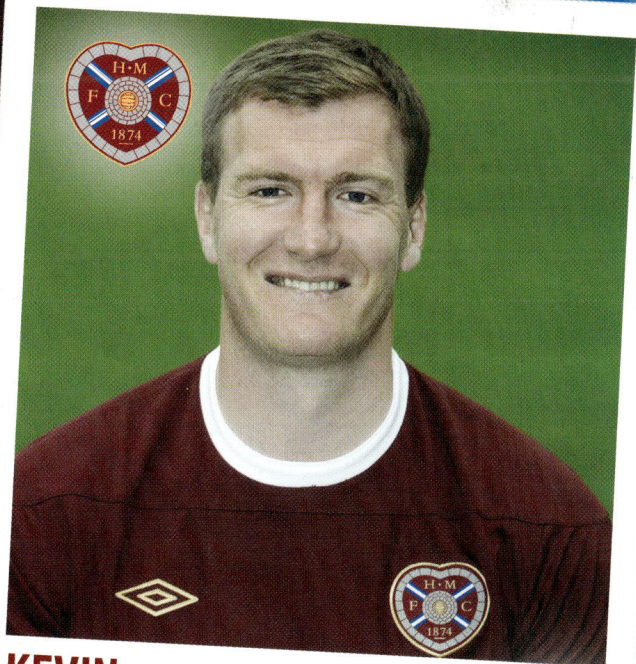

**KEVIN
KYLE**

9

When the hosts grabbed the lead in the second half, it appeared as if Hearts would be returning from Leith empty-handed but the Jambos had other ideas with Elliott's equaliser sending the travelling fans wild with delight.

"I have never been so nervous in a long time with the way the game went," added Kevin. "Going a goal up and cruising then having Marius sent off and suddenly it's 1-1. They then went 2-1 up and I honestly couldn't see us getting back into it.

"But then Andy Webster did well at the back post with a header and when we won another free-kick out wide I was saying to Craig Thomson just put it to the back stick, Webby will win it and hopefully somebody will be there to tap it in.

"Sure enough Stephen Elliott was there – I just jumped up and went crazy!

"The sadness in the eyes of the Hibs fans was a memorable picture and it felt like a point gained rather than two lost."

The experience of the derby as a spectator compared favourably to being involved as a player for big Kevin, who added: "It was nice being part of a win at Easter Road as a Hearts player but it was also nice to be there experiencing it with the fans.

"I was there with Eggert but was a nervous wreck! I didn't think I'd be like that but the club has obviously got a grip on me.

"I have been at an Old Firm game as a neutral to experience it and the noise level was something else. I've played in the Sunderland-Newcastle derby and I don't think that will be beaten in my career because of the size of the crowd.

"The Hibs-Hearts game was like that but on a smaller scale. It was pretty amazing. It's always nice to see the other side go home upset and crying - that's what makes a derby!"

9

10 Classy Captains

HEART OF MIDLOTHIAN FC

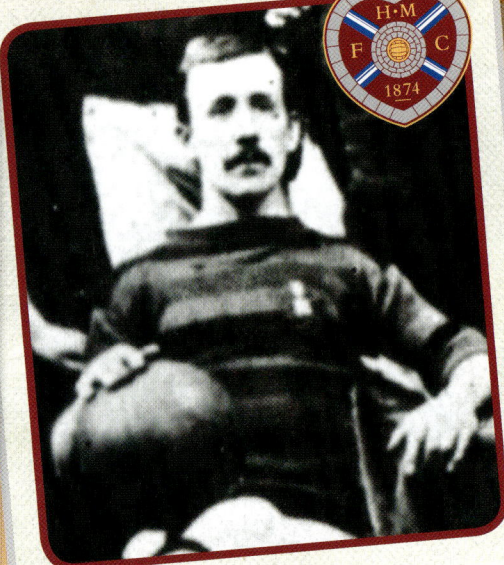

Tom Purdie
1874 - 1881

HEART OF MIDLOTHIAN FC

HEART

Tom Purdie

In 1874, the original Hearts players held a football competition to decide who would be the first captain and the winner was Tom Purdie, who would hold the position until 1881.

He was born in Edinburgh in 1854 and during his playing days, Tom usually operated as a full-back where his fearless tackling and long clearances were much admired. As captain, he also conducted training sessions and Tom was a significant figure in the rise of Hearts from being a public park side to a club that attracted thousands of spectators to private fields at Powburn, Powderhall and then the first Tynecastle.

In April 1878, Tom was the man who led the club to its first trophy success, Hearts beating Hibs in the Edinburgh FA Cup Final after five gruelling matches. Then in May 1879, he skippered the team to victory in the President's Cup Final against Hanover. The following year, Hearts became the first Edinburgh club to challenge the all-conquering Queens Park and Tom was still captain in January 1881 when the Maroons became the first capital side to play in England, against Aston Villa.

In the late 1880s, Tom lived for a spell in London and was on the committee of Tottenham Hotspur. However, he returned home and spent most of his working life at the Castle Mills rubber works. He served on Hearts' committee in the 1890s and eventually became a director. Tom was awarded life membership of the club in August 1927 but passed away in December 1929.

Isaac Begbie

Isaac Begbie was a redoubtable figure in the middle of the park and Hearts' team of the 1890s responded to his ball-winning ability and relentless drive. The supporters also regarded him as a local hero because Isaac was born in Edinburgh in 1868 and lived at his parents' dairy, located on the present site of the Tivoli in Gorgie Road.

Isaac joined Hearts in August 1888 from Dalry Albert and gave the club wonderful service, playing just over 425 matches and starring in the first golden era. In addition, he represented Scotland on four occasions and played for the Scottish Football League three times. Isaac was captain during the first season of League football (1890-91) and indeed, he scored Hearts' first ever goal in this competition. He then led Hearts to its first national honour when Dumbarton was beaten in the Scottish FA Cup Final in February 1891.

The rugged half-back became one of the club's first professional players in 1893 and he was a key man when Hearts beat Hibs in the Scottish Cup Final in 1896. Isaac was also prominent in the splendid sides that won the Scottish League Championship in 1894-95 and 1896-97 and he was actually captain of the first title winners. In addition, during his long career, Isaac won many local honours in competitions such as the East of Scotland Shield and the Rosebery Charity Cup. In August 1900, Isaac signed for Leith Athletic, together with Willie Taylor, for a joint transfer fee of £30. He later played for Bathgate and Falkirk, and passed away in September 1958.

Charlie Thomson
1898 - 1908
HEART OF MIDLOTHI

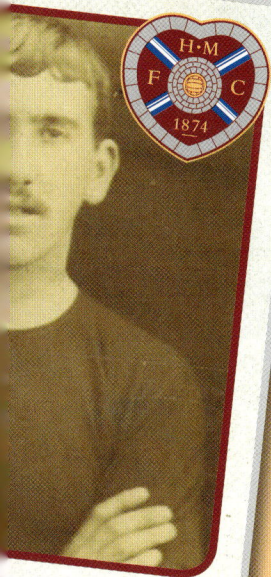

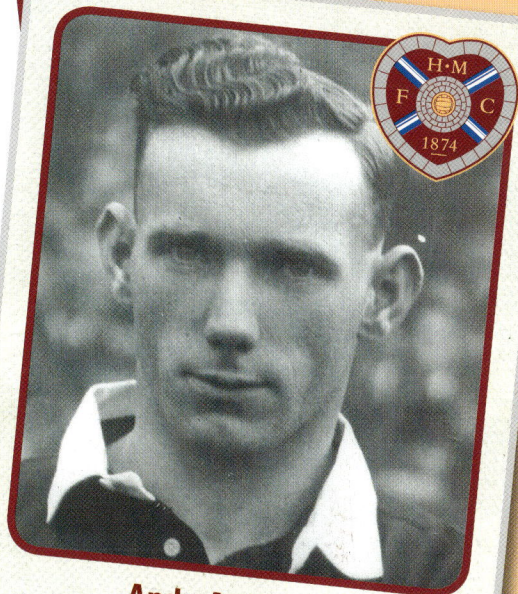

gbie
900
OTHIAN FC

Andy Anderson
1929 - 1946
HEART OF MIDLOTHIAN FC

Charlie Thomson

Although he was originally a centre-forward, Charlie Thomson became Britain's finest centre-half where his physical presence and leadership skills were second to none. In his time, a centre-half always moved forward to prime the attack and he was majestic in this role. As a result, Charlie captained Scotland on a regular basis and 12 of his 21 international appearances came during his time at Tynecastle. In addition, he represented the Scottish League on five occasions.

Charlie was born in 1878 and signed in April 1898 from his home-town junior club, Prestonpans Athletic. A baker to trade, his popularity was assured when he scored in Hearts' 4-3 victory over Celtic in the 1901 Scottish Cup Final. He was unlucky to be on the losing side in the 1903 Final against Rangers but his masterful use of the ball was recognised by his appointment as captain the following year. Hearts' burly skipper also caused opponents problems at set pieces and he scored nearly 125 goals in almost 425 appearances.

He led Hearts to another Scottish Cup victory in 1906 when Third Lanark was defeated 1-0 in the Final and Charlie's absence through injury is reckoned to have cost Hearts a win in the 1907 Final against Celtic. On 27 April 1908, Charlie moved to Sunderland with Tom Allan for £700 and he subsequently inspired the Roker Park side to the English Championship in 1913 and also to the FA Cup Final. Although he played for St Bernards during the Great War in 1916, Charlie had bought the Black Bull in Prestonpans and he retired in 1919 to run his business. Charlie died in February 1936.

Andy Anderson

Andy Anderson was probably the finest full-back to have played for Hearts and that is underlined by his 23 appearances for Scotland and four games for the Scottish League. The brave and sure-footed defender was born in Airdrie in February 1909 and came to Hearts' attention while playing for Baillieston. He was subsequently signed in September 1929 for £100, although this fee was not paid until Baillieston reverted to junior status in 1931. Andy made his debut in January 1930 and immediately became Hearts' first-choice right-back for ten years, playing almost 500 matches.

He was at his best in high pressure games which guaranteed his Scotland place throughout the 30s. When Andy made his international debut against England in April 1933, the Scots won 2-1 before a world record attendance of 134,170 and a feature of the game was his tackling and his coolness during the hottest of English raids.

Andy captained Scotland on several occasions and took over as skipper of Hearts in December 1935. Unfortunately, he won no major club honours, although Andy played in three Scottish Cup Semi-Finals and also helped Hearts to runners-up position in the Scottish League in 1937-38, and the Wartime East & North Division in 1939-40.

A joiner to trade, Andy won the respect of all his opponents with his defensive strength and tenacity. He was an Air Raid Warden at the start of the Second World War and retired from playing in May 1941, being formally released in April 1946.

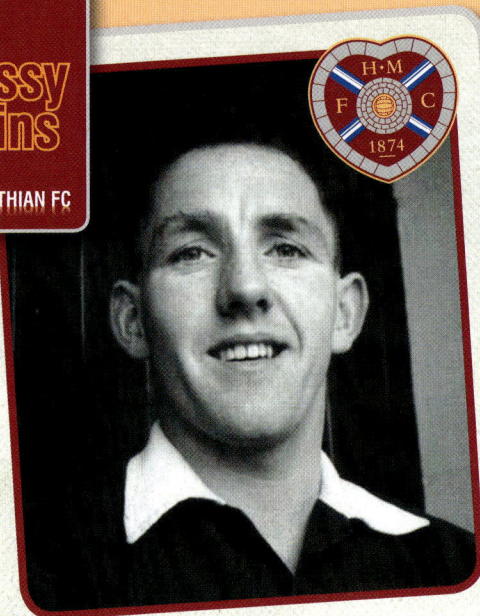

Dave Mackay
1952 - 1959
HEART OF MIDLOTHIAN FC

John Cumming
1948 - 1967
HEART OF MIDLOTHIAN FC

Dave Mackay

Possibly the most complete midfield player that Scotland has ever produced, Dave was a tough ball-winner, a skilled passer and a regular goal scorer. He also had leadership qualities and many believe that his spirit and drive turned Hearts into winners.

Born in Edinburgh in November 1934, the Schoolboy Internationalist was provisionally signed from the juvenile side, Slateford Athletic. Dave was then farmed out to Newtongrange Star, and the apprentice joiner earned Junior international caps before being called up by Hearts in April 1952. He quickly established his place and was outstanding in the team that ended a 48-year-old drought by winning the League Cup in October 1954 against Motherwell. This was followed by victory over Celtic in the Scottish Cup Final in 1956 and the record breaking League Championship success in 1957-58, when Dave was captain of Hearts. It was hardly surprising that he was Scotland's Player of the Year in 1958 and was in the national squad that played at the World Cup Finals in Sweden. Dave appeared for his country on 22 occasions, four while with Hearts, and he also played for the national U23 and "B" teams, and the Scottish League. He was in the Hearts side that won the League Cup Final against Partick Thistle in October 1958, but was then transferred to Tottenham Hotspur in March 1959 for a fee of £32,000. Dave won League and FA Cup medals with Spurs, and had further success with Derby County before starting a splendid managerial career that peaked with Derby becoming English Champions in 1975. Dave also worked in the Middle East but sadly he never managed his favourite club. Nevertheless, he thrilled Hearts fans on the field, scoring 32 goals in 208 games that included the club's first European ventures.

John Cumming

During an illustrious career, John Cumming made 612 appearances for Hearts, scoring 58 goals, and he was a driving force in the teams that won the Scottish Championship in 1957-58 and 1959-60; and the Scottish League Cup in 1954-55, 1958-59, 1959-60 and 1962-63. His contribution was remarkable and John also inspired Hearts to win the Scottish Cup in 1956, and took part in Hearts' first European campaigns.

He was born in Carluke in March 1930 and the ex-miner played for Castlehill Colliery before moving to Carluke Rovers from whom he was provisionally signed by Hearts in 1948. John did his National Service and in January 1950 he signed full-time, with Carluke Rovers receiving a fee of £105. John played on the left-wing until 1953 when he moved to left-back and then any half-back position. John was renowned for his fearless and resolute tackling, while his never-say-die attitude always inspired his colleagues.

His spirit was epitomised in the Scottish Cup Final against Celtic in 1956 when he was a hero, despite concussion and having to leave the field to have stitches inserted in a gashed forehead. At the peak of his career, John earned nine caps for Scotland; seven for the Scottish League; and two for the Scotland "B" team. Hearts' skipper over many seasons was so adaptable that he was once reserve for Scotland in all three half-back positions.

During the club's many overseas tours, John represented Hearts with distinction and when he stopped playing in May 1967, he was appointed trainer. John retired in 1976 and he richly deserved his testimonial in May 1980 as he was a wonderful club servant and one of the greatest men ever to wear a maroon shirt.

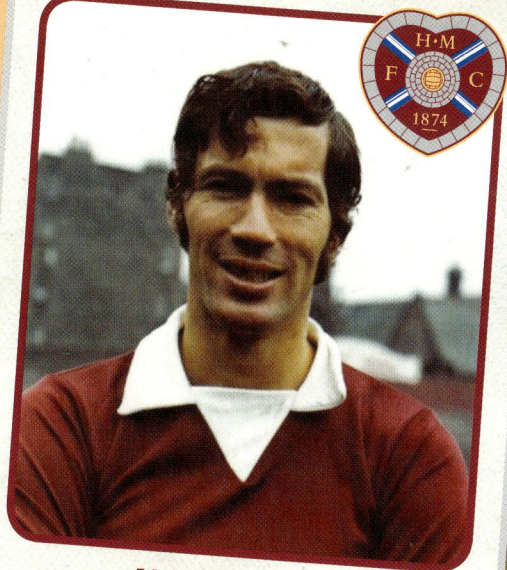

Alan Anderson
1963 - 1976

HEART OF MIDLOTHIAN FC

Dave McPherson
1987 - 1992 & 1994 - 1999

HEART OF MIDLOTHIAN FC

Alan Anderson

Born in Edinburgh in December 1939, Alan is a lifelong Hearts supporter who was immensely proud to captain the club over many years. His playing days started with United Crossroads Boys Club and the muscular defender briefly appeared for Dalkeith Thistle Juniors and Falkirk, before transferring to Millwall in September 1959.

While in London, Alan finished his apprenticeship as a compositor and in 1961-62 he helped Millwall to win the Fourth Division Championship.

In July 1962 the rugged centre-half signed for Scunthorpe United but he never settled and in November 1963, at the age of 24, Alan came to Hearts for £1,500.

The 6'1" defender became one of the club's most admired players, being a formidable obstacle for opponents and particularly strong in the air. He was also a great servant, playing nearly 550 times for Hearts.

Alan had presence at set pieces and he scored 37 goals but like so many of our fine players, he was always a runner-up, appearing in the 1968 Scottish Cup Final; the 1971 Texaco Cup Final; and being a member of the squad that lost the Championship on goal average in 1964-65.

Alan played for Hearts in the New York Soccer League in 1964 and the inspiring defender saw European action in 1965-66.

He represented Scotland seven times on the SFA World Tour in 1967 and also assisted Hearts into the initial Premier Division. Big Alan Anderson retired in May 1976 to pursue a successful career as a publican and hotelier and he remains proud to represent the club at special events.

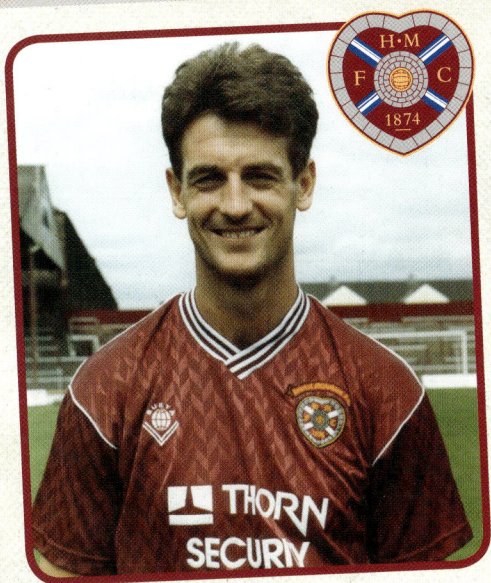

Dave McPherson

Dave was outstanding during two spells with Hearts and the team revolved around the giant centre-half who was born in Paisley in January 1964. He started with Rangers in November 1980 and quickly earned a Championship and two League Cup winners' medals, as well as gaining European experience. However, the U21 internationalist was uncertain of his future and in July 1987, he moved to Hearts for £325,000. He dominated the rearguard and ensured that Hearts finished second in the League in 1987-88. Next season, the Maroons reached the quarter-finals of the UEFA Cup and significantly, Dave was identified as Hearts' most important player by all the European opponents. He also won the first of 27 Scottish caps, 20 while a Hearts player. Dave was appointed captain in 1989-90 and the fans were proud to see him play at the World Cup Finals in Italy. He then led Hearts to second place in the League in 1991-92, before Rangers lured him back to Glasgow in June 1992 for £1.35 million.

After a second spell at Ibrox, "Slim" had gained eight winner's medals and he made a welcome return to Hearts in October 1994 in an exchange deal involving Alan McLaren. Dave was again the cornerstone of the defence which ensured that Hearts regularly played in Europe. He also inspired the team to the Scottish Cup Final in 1996 but an ankle injury kept Dave out of the League Cup Final the following season. After recovering from knee surgery, Dave took his place at right-back when Hearts won the Scottish Cup in 1998 against Rangers. That day, he was a giant in every sense of the word. In 1999, he left for the Carlton Soccer Club in Australia after scoring 37 goals in 416 appearances. Dave returned home to sign for Morton in August 2001. He later coached at Morton and also in Australia.

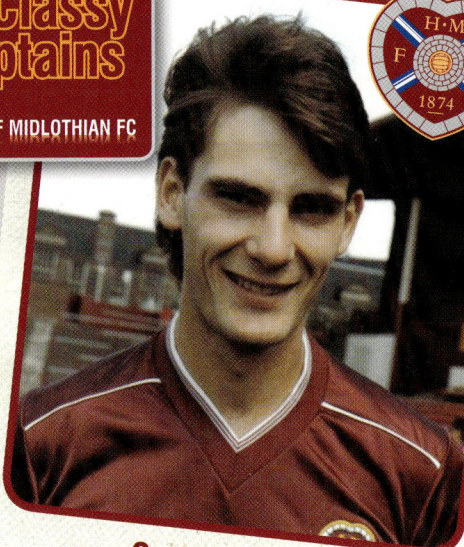

10 Classy Captains
HEART OF MIDLOTHIAN FC

Craig Levein
1983 - 1997 & 2000 - 2004
HEART OF MIDLOTHIAN FC

Steven Pressley
1998 - 2006
HEART OF MIDLOTHIAN FC

Craig Levein

A Fifer from Aberdour, Craig Levein was born in October 1964, and the majestic stopper would have become the finest sweeper in Britain had he not suffered a series of terrible knee injuries.

The cool and assured defender played for Lochore Welfare Juniors before joining Cowdenbeath and then moving to Hearts in November 1983 for an initial fee of £30,000. Craig was the SPFA Young Player of the Year in both 1984 and 1985, and a star man as Hearts came so close to the League and Cup "double" in 1985-86.

However, he had to rebuild his career after two knee operations but did so in style and became an established Scottish international, earning 16 caps and playing at the 1990 World Cup Finals.

With his strength, pace and skill on the ball, Craig became Hearts captain and twice helped the club to runners-up position in the League. Sadly, however, he was to suffer two further knee injuries and was forced to give up playing in May 1997 after 462 games for Hearts.

Craig coached at Livingston before taking over as manager of Cowdenbeath in November 1997 and driving his local club to become Third Division promotion contenders. He then became Hearts manager in December 2000 and guided the club to third place in the Premier League in successive seasons.

Hearts also played regularly in Europe before Craig went to Leicester City in October 2004. After a spell at Raith Rovers, he was appointed manager of Dundee United in October 2006 and Craig revived the fortunes of the club before becoming the manager of Scotland in December 2009.

Steven Pressley

A tough, assured and experienced centre-back, Steven was an inspirational Hearts captain. He was also a regular in the international team and is the most capped player in the club's history, having appeared 32 times for Scotland. Steven was born in Elgin in October 1973 but he was raised in Fife and joined Rangers in 1990 from Inverkeithing Boys Club. The six-foot defender earned Championship and Scottish Cup medals while at Ibrox and gained considerable European experience before joining Coventry City in October 1994.

Steven then signed for Dundee United in July 1995 and his resolute defending helped the club to finish third in the Premier Division and reach the League Cup Final. Steven's consistency also earned further U21 caps and he gained a remarkable 27 at this level. Jim Jefferies was attracted to his style and when his contract expired in July 1998, Steven signed for Hearts. He played in a number of positions, but after settling in central defence, Steven became a huge player for Hearts, taking over as captain and defensive co-ordinator in August 2001.

He subsequently helped Hearts to finish third in the League on three occasions and to establish a regular presence in the UEFA Cup where it would be difficult to match his personal performance in that famous victory in Bordeaux in November 2003. Steven's career reached a new high in 2005-06 when he scored the first kick in the penalty shoot-out that brought victory over Gretna in the Scottish Cup Final. In addition, he inspired the team to claim second position in the SPL and a Champions League qualification place. Steven signed for Celtic in December 2006 and then after spells with Randers and Falkirk, he moved into coaching, first with the national team and then Falkirk.

Find the names of 10 of Hearts' European opponents. Answers on page 59.

BORDEAUX
BAYERN
BRAGA
STUTTGART
ZELJEZNICAR
SCHALKE
AEK ATHENS
LANTANA
FERENCVAROS
BASEL

WORDSEARCH

S	X	S	N	E	H	T	A	K	E	A	Z
O	U	C	B	Y	L	N	Z	J	L	X	E
R	A	S	W	R	N	W	K	V	C	K	L
A	E	Q	T	N	W	S	P	L	V	H	J
V	D	X	M	U	C	K	W	Q	K	R	E
C	R	Y	A	H	T	Y	W	X	T	T	Z
N	O	R	A	N	N	T	M	L	K	G	N
E	B	L	L	R	A	L	G	T	N	L	I
R	K	D	E	H	M	T	T	A	E	L	C
E	N	Y	M	Z	R	M	N	S	R	M	A
F	A	K	K	K	B	Q	A	A	H	T	R
B	B	R	A	G	A	G	A	B	X	V	L	G	W

Marius Zaliukas

26

QUIZ ANSWERS

P23 SPOT THE BALL

P32 QUIZ

1. 2002-03
2. Colin Cameron
3. Antwerp
4. Wolves
5. St Johnstone
6. Australian
7. Craig Levein
8. Bayern Munich
9. False. Andy was born in Dundee
10. 1886

P46 GUESS WHO?

1. Paulo Sergio
2. Arvydas Novikovas
3. Ryan McGowan

P28 MAZE

P42 WORD SEARCH

Y	G	E	N	O	B	T	D	L	H
S	M	Z	L	C	H	E	M	N	K
E	A	T	D	K	V	F	O	R	D
L	D	T	H	R	K	S	I	K	N
T	A	C	I	N	T	K	C	R	J
T	D	E	O	R	L	D	R	N	Y
A	S	L	E	N	Q	G	A	M	Z
B	K	B	U	M	N	X	B	B	J
M	O	G	T	A	T	J	B	V	Y
R	Y	D	D	M	B	N	E	Q	J

P57 WORD SEARCH

S	X	S	N	E	H	T	A	K	E	A	Z
O	U	C	B	Y	L	N	Z	J	L	X	E
R	A	S	W	R	N	W	K	V	C	K	L
A	E	Q	T	N	W	S	P	L	V	H	J
V	D	X	M	U	C	K	W	Q	K	R	E
C	R	Y	A	H	T	Y	W	X	T	T	Z
N	O	R	A	N	N	T	M	L	K	G	N
E	B	L	L	R	A	L	G	T	N	L	I
R	K	D	E	H	M	T	T	A	E	L	C
E	N	Y	M	Z	R	M	N	S	R	M	A
F	A	K	K	K	B	Q	A	A	H	T	R
B	B	R	A	G	A	B	X	V	L	G	W

59

HEART OF MIDLOTHIAN WOMEN AND GIRLS FC WAS OFFICIALLY UNVEILED AT A CEREMONY AT TYNECASTLE STADIUM IN AUGUST 2009 – AND ALREADY IT IS A FORCE TO BE RECKONED WITH.

HEARTS WOMEN

DURING 2010 HEARTS WOMEN REACHED THE QUARTER-FINAL OF THE SCOTTISH CUP AND, THAT SAME YEAR, THE U17S – WHO BOAST FOUR PLAYERS IN THE SOUTH-EAST SCOTLAND REGIONAL SQUAD - WERE RUNNERS-UP IN THEIR REGIONAL LEAGUE CUP FINAL.

A League Cup final appearance was also among the achievements of the U13s – again in 2010 – who began their 2011 campaign with a long unbeaten run.

For the U15s, meanwhile, the 2010 season saw them lead the league for all but the last two weeks, at which point they were pipped to the title by three points. Needless to say, their 2011 season has also been full of promise.

The club is affiliated to the Scottish Women's Football Association, part of the Scottish FA, and is benefiting from the rise in popularity of the women's game, which was thrillingly demonstrated during the World Cup Finals, held in Germany during the summer, played in front of packed stadia and culminating in a final that went to a penalty shoot-out between victors Japan and the USA.

As well as aspiring towards excellence on the football field, the club seeks also to provide an important social function for girls and women: a mix of fun and self-discipline, ambition and skills development, fitness and friendship.

The club has already been accredited by the Scottish FA as a Quality Mark Development Club, having met standards including coach/player ratio, child protection policy and insurance.

To rival the commitment required in the boys' and men's game, all teams at Hearts train at least twice a week.

Says club chair, Margaret Milne: "Our club, like others, works towards creating a pathway for girls to progress through the age groups and we work towards having the players playing at their optimum level.

"For example, we have a girl who has moved straight from playing U15s football last season into our ladies team, based on her ability and attitude and she has done very well at that level and we feel that it will assist with her own personal progress in the game."

Striving towards finding a single home venue to call their own, the club play across a variety of locations: Musselburgh Athletic's Olivebank, for the women; Dalkeith Community Campus, for the U17s and U15s; and Meadowmill, for the U13s.

Also among the club's more immediate ambitions is to set up a junior section, catering for ages six to 11, to provide a steady stream of accomplished players into the U13 set-up.

But at the other end of the age spectrum from the women's team, mention must be made of captain Kim Borthwick (pictured below with Gary Locke), a prolific goalscorer from midfield who is training to become a PE teacher.

Adds the club chair: "Kim is a fantastic role model. She has represented Scotland at both U17 and U19 levels and is a lovely, responsible young woman. She is a great footballer and a great person."

The 2012 season is scheduled to begin in March.

The club would like to thank, among others, its sponsors large and small, including Women's team sponsors Independent Plant Services Ltd, plus Action Scaffolding Limited, Baberton Building Services, Howdens Joinery (Sighthill), MKM Building Supplies, MSL (Scotland) Ltd, Stevenswood Windows and Wiseman Dairies.

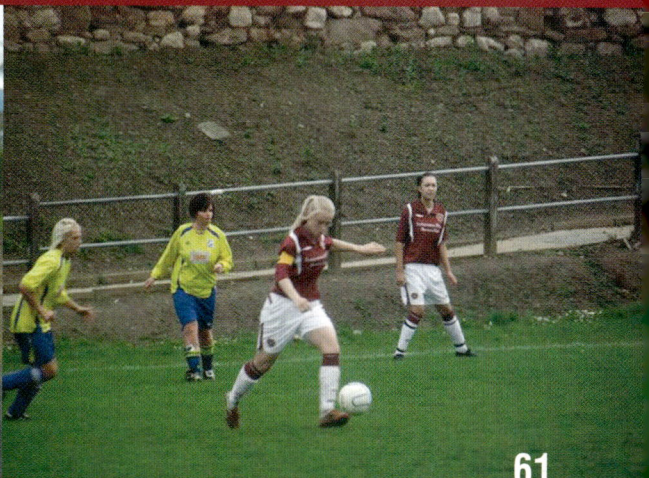